Harlem
Renaissance

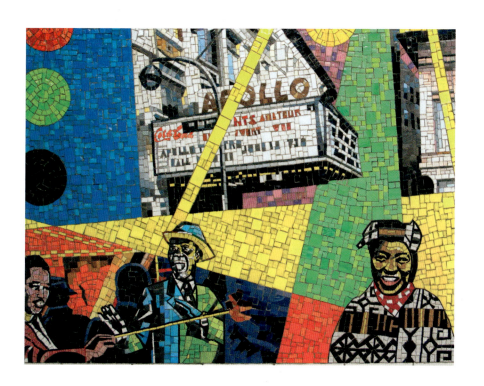

THIS EDITION

Editorial Management by Oriel Square
Produced for DK by WonderLab Group LLC
Jennifer Emmett, Erica Green, Kate Hale, *Founders*

Editor Maya Myers; **Photography Editor** Nicole DiMella; **Managing Editor** Rachel Houghton; **Designers** Project Design Company; **Researcher** Michelle Harris; **Copy Editor** Lori Merritt; **Indexer** Connie Binder; **Proofreader** Susan K. Hom; **Sensitivity Reader** Ebonye Gussine Wilkins; **Series Reading Specialist** Dr. Jennifer Albro

First American Edition, 2024
Published in the United States by DK Publishing, a division of Penguin Random House LLC
1745 Broadway, 20th Floor, New York, NY 10019

Copyright © 2024 Dorling Kindersley Limited
24 25 26 27 10 9 8 7 6 5 4 3 2 1
001–339804–Jun/2024

All rights reserved.
Without limiting the rights under the copyright reserved above, no part of this publication may be reproduced, stored in or introduced into a retrieval system, or transmitted, in any form, or by any means (electronic, mechanical, photocopying, recording, or otherwise), without the prior written permission of the copyright owner.
Published in Great Britain by Dorling Kindersley Limited

A catalog record for this book is available from the Library of Congress.
HC ISBN: 978-07440-9456-5
PB ISBN: 978-07440-9453-4

DK books are available at special discounts when purchased in bulk for sales promotions, premiums, fund-raising, or educational use.
For details, contact:
DK Publishing Special Markets, 1745 Broadway, 20th Floor, New York, NY 10019
SpecialSales@dk.com

Printed and bound in China

The publisher would like to thank the following for their kind permission to reproduce their images:
a=above; c=center; b=below; l=left; r=right; t=top; b/g=background

Alamy Stock Photo: Chronicle 35tl, Cinematic Collection 43cr, Classicpaintings 28br (Background), © The Estate of Vincent Smith, courtesy Alexandre Gallery, New York / Randy Duchaine 1b, Everett Collection Historical 28tl, Everett Collection Inc 23crb, IanDagnall Computing 27tl, North Wind Picture Archives 10t, Science History Images 20tr, 28br, Science History Images / Photo Researchers 39t, WorldPhotos 38r, ZUMA Press, Inc. 42; **Bridgeman Images:** Bearden, Romare Howard (1911-88) / American © Romare Bearden Foundation / VAGA at ARS, NY and DACS, London 2024 29, Chicago History Museum / © Estate of Archibald John Motley Jr. All reserved rights 2023 / Valerie Gerrard Browne 9cra, 20, Jacob Lawrence (1917-2000) / American © The Jacob and Gwendolyn Knight Lawrence Foundation, Seattle / Artists Rights Society (ARS), New York and DACS, London 2024 12b, 25b, Van Der Zee, James (1886-1983) / American Minneapolis Institute of Art / The Stanley Hawks Memorial Fund 27b; **Carl Van Vechten photograph © VanVechtenTrust:** ©Van Vechten Trust/Carl Van Vechten Papers Relating to African American Arts and Letters. James Weldon Johnson Collection in the Yale Collection of American Literature, Beinecke Rare Book and Manuscript Library 26br; **Collection of the Smithsonian National Museum of African American History and Culture:** 37crb, 40cl, Gift from Dawn Simon Spears and Alvin Spears, Sr. 40br; **Dorling Kindersley:** Musee du Louvre, Paris / Philippe Sebert 8br; **Dreamstime.com:** Denis Barbulat 17tr (Background), 31tc (Background), Demerzel21 15, Iofoto 41, Vadim Kozlovsky 14tr (Background), 18crb (Background), 19tl (Background), 23cra (Background), 27tl (Background), 33crb (Background), 35tl (Background); **Getty Images:** Archive Photos / Fotosearch 15bl, Archive Photos / Hulton Archive 22cl, Archive Photos / Transcendental Graphics 36-37, Bettmann 30b, 31tc, 41tr, Chicago History Museum / Archive Photos 13t, Gamma-Keystone / Keystone-France 34b, 45t, Heritage Images / Hulton Archive 21cr, Marian 14 (Background), 18-19 (Background), 22-23 (Background), 27 (Background), 32-35 (Background), 40, Michael Ochs Archives 31br, New York Daily News 9t, Scott Olson 17bl, Redferns / Gilles Petard 32t, Redferns / JP Jazz Archive 22br, The New York Historical Society / Archive Photos 7t, Transcendental Graphics 37tl, Universal Images Group 3cb, 6cl, Donna Ward 43bl; **Getty Images / iStock:** Olya Solodenko 32t (background), 40cl (Background), Sololos 22cl (Background), 24clb (Background), 35crb (Background); **Library of Congress, Washington, D.C.:** Gottlieb, William P. Portrait of Billie Holiday, Downbeat, New York, N.Y., ca. Feb. United States, 1947. , Monographic. Photograph. https: / / www.loc.gov / item / gottlieb.04251 / . 33crb, LC-DIG-ds-00894 / Underwood & Underwood 16b, LC-USF34-018201-E / Dorothea Lange 13crb, LC-USZ61-1854 / Marcus Garvey, -1940. , 1924. Aug. 5. Photograph. https: / / www.loc. gov / item / 2003653533 / . 19tl, LC-USZ62-42507 / Carl Van Vechten, photographer. Portrait of Romare Bearden. , 1944. Photograph. https: / / www.loc.gov / item / 2004662578 / . 29cr; **National Portrait Gallery, Smithsonian Institution:** 17tr, 18crb, 35crb; **The New York Public Library:** Schomburg Center for Research in Black Culture, Art and Artifacts Division, The New York Public Library. "Aspects of Negro Life" The New York Public Library Digital Collections. 1934. https: / / digitalcollections.nypl.org / items / 6ca557ed-9597-5dcd-e040-e00a18065af4 28tl (Background), Schomburg Center for Research in Black Culture, Jean Blackwell Hutson Research and Reference Division, The New York Public Library. "Front cover" The New York Public Library Digital Collections. 1923-04. https: / / digitalcollections.nypl.org / items / b9f2b588-8fbe-d39b-e040-e00a180679bc 24tr, Schomburg Center for Research in Black Culture, Photographs and Prints Division, The New York Public Library. "Portrait of Arthur Alfonso Schomburg, bibliophile" The New York Public Library Digital Collections. 1900 - 1935. https: / / digitalcollections.nypl.org / items / 84c3b888-cab5-3fb6-e040-e00a180660fa 11b, 14tr, 24clb, 26t; **Newspapers.com:** The New York Age / Philip Payton Jr. Company advertisement 15t; **Shutterstock.com:** Here Now 44-45b, Roman Nogin 4-5; **Yale University Library:** Wallace Thurman Collection. Yale Collection of American Literature, Beinecke Rare Book and Manuscript Library. 22-23tc

Cover images: *Front:* **Alamy Stock Photo:** IanDagnall Computing br; **Getty Images:** Archive Photos / Fotosearch / Stringer bc, Library of Congress / Corbis Historical cla, Michael Ochs Archives bl, Redferns / Gilles Petard cr, Redferns / JP Jazz Archive crb; **Getty Images / iStock:** Sololos (Background); *Back:* **Dreamstime.com:** Furtseff cra; **The New York Public Library:** Schomburg Center for Research in Black Culture, Jean Blackwell Hutson Research and Reference Division, The New York Public Library. "Front cover" The New York Public Library Digital Collections. 1923-04. https: / / digitalcollections.nypl.org / items / b9f2b588-8fbe-d39b-e040-e00a180679bc cl

All other images © Dorling Kindersley
For more information see: www.dkimages.com

www.dk.com

This book was made with Forest Stewardship Council™ certified paper – one small step in DK's commitment to a sustainable future.
Learn more at
www.dk.com/uk/information/sustainability

Harlem
Renaissance

Melissa H. Mwai

Contents

6	The Dreamer of Harlem
8	Heading to Harlem
10	The History of Harlem
16	Changes Coming in Harlem
21	Culture Blooms in Harlem
42	Harlem Goes On
46	Glossary
47	Index
48	Quiz

The Dreamer of Harlem

It was a bright September morning in 1921. A young Black man named Langston Hughes stepped off the subway at 135th Street in Harlem, a neighborhood in New York City. All around him, Black folks were on their way to work. Langston was excited. He wanted to shake hands with everyone who passed by.

Langston was very happy to be living in Harlem. The Jazz Age was in full swing. He had gotten to see the famous singer Florence Mills in *Shuffle Along* at the Cort Theater. It was, he later wrote, "a honey of a show."

The neighborhood was rich with Black art and Black artists. It seemed like a celebration of Black culture was blossoming around every corner.

Langston's dream was to become a famous writer. And he felt sure that Harlem was the place where he could make that dream come true.

Heading to Harlem

In the early 1900s, Harlem was known as the Black capital of America. Like Hughes, many people wanted to be part of the largest Black community in the US.

Many people moved to Harlem for a new beginning. Black people in the US faced unfair treatment because of their skin color. This is known as racism. This was especially true in southern states, where slavery had once been common. Laws separated Black and white people in public. This was called segregation.

The Other Renaissance
From the 14th to the 17th centuries, people in Europe made advances in knowledge, science, and art. This time is known as "the Renaissance."

There was segregation and racism in Harlem, too. However, the supportive community there made life better. Churches and community centers helped newcomers. Black businesses served everyone. Over time, Black life and culture thrived in Harlem.

The time from the end of World War I through the 1930s is known as the Harlem Renaissance [reh-nuh-SAHNTS]. Renaissance means "rebirth." During the Harlem Renaissance, Black people changed their culture in exciting ways.

The History of Harlem

Before there were brick buildings and busy streets, Harlem was farmland. The Lenape people lived and traveled there.

In the 1600s, Dutch settlers claimed this land by "buying" it from the Lenape. The Lenape believed they were sharing the land, but the Dutch believed it now belonged to them. The Dutch named their village Nieuw Haarlem, after a city in the Netherlands. Later, the name changed to Harlem.

Beginning at the end of the 19th century, millions of people immigrated to the US. Many people came to New York City. The city's population exploded. Harlem was less crowded than some parts of the city. So, some immigrants moved there.

But from 1893 to 1896, the American government lost a lot of money. People lost their jobs and homes. Many white people moved out of Harlem. This made room for a new community to grow.

From the 1910s to the 1970s, about six million Black people moved out of the American South. Since the Civil War, life for Black people in the South had been difficult. It was hard for them to get jobs that paid well. In the North, they could build railroads or work in factories. So, many Black people moved to northern cities, like Chicago, Detroit, and New York. This period of movement was called the Great Migration. Many of these people moved to Harlem.

The Migration Series, Panel No. 3,
Jacob Lawrence, circa 1940

Unfair Farming

After slavery ended, some laws made it difficult for Black people to own land. Some white landowners rented land or tools to white and Black farmers. The farmers paid the landowners with crops that they grew. This was called sharecropping. Sharecropping deals were often unfair to the farmers. Sometimes it was impossible for farmers to pay what they owed. This made it very hard for the farmers to get out of these arrangements.

Philip A. Payton Jr.
(1876–1917)

One person played a big part in building up the Black community in Harlem. Philip A. Payton Jr. ran rental businesses for white landlords there. He wrote newspaper ads encouraging Black people to rent homes. In 1904, Payton started the Afro-American Realty Company. It helped Black people fight for fair rent prices. It lessened racism against Black renters. Payton became known as "the father of Harlem."

While new Black residents were more welcome in Harlem, the Great Migration was not as well received in other places. And trouble in other places would bring change to Harlem, too.

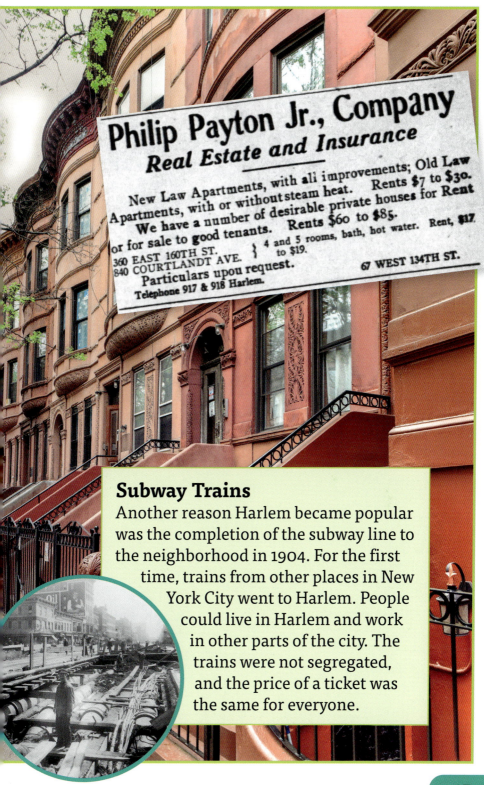

Philip Payton Jr., Company
Real Estate and Insurance

New Law Apartments, with all improvements; Old Law Apartments, with or without steam heat. Rents $7 to $30.
We have a number of desirable private houses for Rent or for sale to good tenants. Rents $60 to $85.

360 EAST 160TH ST. } 4 and 5 rooms, bath, hot water. Rent, $17
840 COURTLANDT AVE.   to $19.
Particulars upon request. 67 WEST 134TH ST.
Telephone 917 & 918 Harlem.

Subway Trains

Another reason Harlem became popular was the completion of the subway line to the neighborhood in 1904. For the first time, trains from other places in New York City went to Harlem. People could live in Harlem and work in other parts of the city. The trains were not segregated, and the price of a ticket was the same for everyone.

Changes Coming in Harlem

On July 2, 1917, a series of violent attacks began in East St. Louis, Illinois. Some white people were angry that so many Black people were moving up from the South. They attacked Black workers as they left work for the day. They burned Black people's homes. After a week, about 200 Black people had been killed.

Weeks later and a thousand miles away, nearly 10,000 people joined a silent march in New York City to protest the attacks in East St. Louis. As racial tensions swelled around the country, a new push for freedom began. And Harlem was home to many leaders of the fight.

W. E. B. Du Bois
(1868–1963)

W. E. B. Du Bois was an activist. An activist works to create social change. Du Bois believed Black and white races were equal. He attended an unsegregated high school. He graduated from Harvard University. He wrote about Black and white people living together. He also wrote to protest segregation of the government under President Woodrow Wilson.

NAACP
In 1909, Du Bois helped to create the National Association for the Advancement of Colored People. As it did then, the organization today demands equality for all and fights against injustice everywhere.

Ida B. Wells-Barnett
(1862–1931)

Ida B. Wells-Barnett was an activist and a journalist. She was born in Mississippi to enslaved parents. In 1892, her friend Thomas Moss, a Black man, was killed by a white mob in Memphis. For the rest of her life, Wells-Barnett wrote articles and gave speeches against attacks like this. Wells-Barnett was a founder of the NAACP. In 1913, she also started the Alpha Suffrage Club, a Black women's club supporting voting rights for women.

Mob Attacks
Between the end of the Civil War and 1950, thousands of Black people were killed by white crowds. These attacks happened mostly in southern states.

Marcus Garvey
(1887–1940)

Marcus Garvey was raised in Jamaica and educated in London before moving to Harlem. He started a restaurant and a newspaper and helped other Black businesses support themselves. Garvey believed that all Black people should live in Africa. He started the Universal Negro Improvement Association, or UNIA. This group believed in Black pride and unity. Garvey made the phrase "Black is beautiful" popular.

Alain Locke
(1885–1954)

In 1924, the writer Alain Locke talked about "The New Negro." Locke believed that many white Americans wanted to keep Black people from succeeding. But now that slavery had ended, Locke thought that Black writers could and should tell new stories about Black life.

Barbeuce, Archibald Motley, circa 1934

Culture Blooms in Harlem

Black leaders shared ideas to make life better. More people moved to Harlem. And the culture of Harlem bloomed. Many of the people we remember from the Harlem Renaissance were leaders in writing, art, music, and sports.

Writing

In the 1920s and 1930s, newspapers and magazines with Black editors published works by Black writers. Even white-owned newspapers reviewed these popular stories.

Langston Hughes
(1901–1967)

Langston Hughes wrote poetry about the regular lives of Black Americans. His first poem, "The Weary Blues," was published in 1925. In the poem, a man sings about being tired and lonely. People understood how this man felt. They liked the poem. Hughes wrote many poems about people of all ages living in Harlem. No wonder he is called "the people's poet"!

Singing the Blues

Blues music was created after the Civil War by Black Americans. It grew out of work songs and spirituals that used a call-and-response pattern.

Fire!!
Langston Hughes and Zora Neale Hurston edited a Black arts magazine called *Fire!!* Ironically, all the existing copies of the magazine were destroyed in a fire.

Zora Neale Hurston
(1891–1960)

As a little girl in Florida, Zora Neale Hurston loved hearing the people in her town tell stories. When she grew up, she started writing stories of her own. In 1925, she moved to Harlem. She entered a magazine's writing contest and won four prizes. She made friends with Langston Hughes and W. E. B. Du Bois. She collected and wrote stories for the rest of her life.

Hurston's novel *Their Eyes Were Watching God* was published in 1937. In her novel and her stories, Hurston imagined equal rights for women.

Effie Lee Newsome
(1885-1979)

Effie Lee Newsome celebrated the lives of Black children in her poems. Newsome edited a children's column in *The Crisis*, a political magazine that started in Harlem.

Arturo Alfonso Schomburg
(1874-1938)

Arturo Alfonso Schomburg was an Afro-Puerto Rican history writer. He collected books about African history. Today, his collection is part of a research library and museum called the Schomburg Center.

Visual Art

Black artists created many great works of art during the Harlem Renaissance. They were inspired by their African roots, popular music, and people in their community.

Black artists could show their work in many places in Harlem. But there was still racism in the art world. Black artists were often paid less than white artists. In 1935, Harlem artists formed a group to support new artists, host art shows, and fight for better pay.

Harlem Street Scene, Jacob Lawrence, 1942 (detail)

Augusta Savage
(1892–1962)

Augusta Savage was a sculptor. Her sculpture *The Harp* was based on the song "Lift Every Voice and Sing." Millions of people admired *The Harp* at the 1939 World's Fair. Sadly, the plaster sculpture, along with the other art from the fair, was destroyed when the fair was over.

In 1938, Savage started the Harlem Community Art Center to support young Black artists. The center provided free or low-cost arts education.

James Van Der Zee (1886–1983)

James Van Der Zee took photographs of regular people in Harlem. Van Der Zee wanted the people to look their best. He gave them flowers and fancy costumes to wear. He even drew sparkly jewelry on the photos!

Van Der Zee took pictures of basketball teams, church groups, and military parades. In 1924, he became the photographer for Marcus Garvey's UNIA.

Aaron Douglas
(1899-1979)

Aaron Douglas moved to Harlem in 1925 to make art for magazines. Douglas mixed modern and African art in his paintings. The paintings used bold shapes and bright colors. He was known as "the father of African American art."

Loïs Mailou Jones
(1905-1998)

Loïs Mailou Jones had her first art exhibit when she was 17. She came to Harlem to study art. Her paintings featured African masks with rich colors and patterns. She also illustrated books for Black children.

Folk Musicians (detail), Romare Bearden, 1942

Romare Bearden (1911–1988)

Romare Bearden was a collage artist and painter. He worked as a social worker in New York City during the day and painted at night. His art showed life in the city as well as scenes from his childhood in the South. Bearden made many paintings. They were shown throughout the US and Europe during his lifetime.

Music and Dance

After World War I, jazz music and dancing became popular in America. This time became known as "the Jazz Age." It played a big part in the Harlem Renaissance. Jazz music was created by Black Americans in New Orleans, Louisiana. As more Black people moved to Harlem, its night clubs became hot spots for jazz.

Changing Times
The energetic spirit of jazz music was new and different. Older people thought jazz music was wild. Young people loved dancing to the fast songs!

Duke Ellington
(1899–1974)

Duke Ellington was a jazz piano player and composer. Ellington led the band at the Cotton Club in Harlem from 1927 to 1931. Recordings and national radio broadcasts of the band's shows made Ellington famous all over the country. He hosted several concerts to raise money for the NAACP. His career lasted for over 50 years.

Club Spotlight

From 1923 to 1935, the Cotton Club was the place to be and be seen in Harlem. Bands played music for people to dance to. The club put on shows with singing, dancing, comedy, and more. Most of the performers were Black. But with very few exceptions, only white customers were allowed at the club.

Bessie Smith
(ca. 1894–1937)

Bessie Smith was known as "the Empress of the Blues." Smith sang about being a Black woman in America. Her first big hit, "Down-Hearted Blues," was recorded in 1923. Audiences liked the way her strong voice told about both good and bad times.

Smith recorded 160 songs in her life. She was the highest-paid Black entertainer in Harlem. She sang with other jazz artists, like Louis Armstrong and Sidney Bechet. Smith was inducted into the Rock and Roll Hall of Fame in 1989.

Billie Holiday
(1915–1959)

Billie Holiday was a popular jazz singer in Harlem in the 1930s. Holiday became the first Black woman to sing with an all-white band. Her most famous song, "Strange Fruit," was about the murders of Black people in front of white crowds. Some people think of this as the first American protest song for equal rights. This song sold a million copies, more than any of Holiday's other records.

Josephine Baker
(1906–1975)

Josephine Baker's dancing and costumes made her famous in both Harlem and Paris, France. During World War II, she sang and danced for troops. But the audience didn't know that Baker was a spy. She passed messages written in invisible ink on her music.

Until her death, Baker fought racism. She refused to perform in places where Black and white people couldn't be together. In 1963, she spoke at the March on Washington with Martin Luther King Jr.

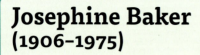

Florence Mills
(1896–1927)

Florence Mills was a star of the stage. She sang and danced in musical shows. People of all races rushed to see her in New York City and in Paris. About 150,000 people attended her funeral in Harlem.

James Weldon Johnson
(1871–1938)

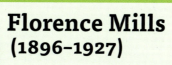

James Weldon Johnson was an activist and a writer. He wrote the lyrics for the song "Lift Every Voice and Sing." The song asked Black people to march for freedom. Since the civil rights movement of the 1960s, it has been known as the Black National Anthem.

Sports

After World War I, Americans wanted to forget the war. Playing sports was one way to do that. The 1920s was known as "the Golden Age of Sports" in the US.

At that time, teams, leagues, and championships were segregated. Black players were on Black teams, and white players were on white teams.

Buck Leonard and James Stark in a Negro League game between the Homestead Grays and the New York Black Yankees

John Henry "Pop" Lloyd (1884–1964)

The Lincoln Stars were a Harlem baseball team. Pop Lloyd was the Stars' best batter and shortstop. In 1913, Lloyd and the Stars won 101 games and lost only six. They beat the Chicago American Giants to win the Negro League championship.

Black vs. White

Black and white teams didn't usually play against each other. But sometimes, they met for extra games. Games between Black and white teams were very popular. Thousands of Black and white fans gathered in the stands to watch. The Stars beat many white teams, including the Philadelphia Phillies, the second-best white team in the country.

Black basketball teams rented out dance floors to play on. The team that played in the Renaissance Ballroom called themselves the Rens. They were the first all-Black, Black-owned professional basketball team in history. Between 1923 and 1947, the Rens won 2,318 games and lost 381.

John Isaacs, also known as Boy Wonder, who signed with the Harlem Rens in 1936

The New York Rens, photographed by James Van Der Zee, 1925

Like the Stars, the Rens defeated many white teams. In 1939, the Rens beat the Oshkosh All-Stars to win the first World Professional Basketball Tournament. The Rens were champions!

> **Women in the Game**
> There were Black sports teams for women as well as for men. In 1913, Edith Trice was a leading player on Harlem's Younger Set basketball team. They played their home games at Young's Casino in Harlem.

Fashion

Some people in Harlem used fashion to display their creativity and pride. In the 1920s, shorter haircuts and hemlines for women made the news.

Madam C. J. Walker
(1867–1919)

In 1905, Madam C. J. Walker spent $1.25 to start a business. She made hair products for Black women. They became very popular. Walker became the first self-made female millionaire in America.

Walker wanted to improve the lives of Black people. She gave thousands of Black women jobs. She gave money to many organizations that supported Black people.

Ann Lowe
(1898-1981)

White-owned stores did not serve Black customers, so Black designers like Ann Lowe opened shops. Lowe designed dresses for all types of women. She designed the wedding dress for future first lady Jackie Kennedy.

Ruby Bailey
(1905-2003)

Ruby Bailey was a dressmaker, painter, and actress. Her family moved from Bermuda to Harlem in 1912. She was famous for patterns and beadwork. Her designs matched the vibrant spirit of Harlem.

Harlem Goes On

The Harlem Renaissance brought a lot of changes. Those changes still affect us today.

Organizations like the NAACP and the Schomburg Center are still active in Harlem. More than a century later, they still work to support the lives of Black people everywhere.

Harlem Renaissance leaders planted the seeds for the civil rights movement of the 1950s and 1960s. This was a time when many Americans fought for equal rights for all people. Those same leaders also inspire Black Lives Matter activists today.

Harlem Renaissance artists and athletes paved the way for future stars. They inspired them, too.

The writer Alice Walker made it her mission to make Zora Neale Hurston's work popular again in the 1970s.

Singers like Janis Joplin and Queen Latifah got song ideas from Bessie Smith.

Queen Latifah as Bessie Smith in the movie *Bessie*

Basketball star Kareem Abdul-Jabbar made a film about the Harlem Rens.

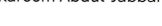

Kareem Abdul-Jabbar

A century ago, Harlem was the place to be. The great leaders and stories from the Harlem Renaissance still inspire today's leaders. People everywhere continue to enjoy the art and ideas that came out of the Harlem Renaissance. The Black leaders of this important time broke new ground. Their stories give people in Harlem, and around the world, hope for tomorrow.

45

Glossary

Activist
A person who works to create social change

Civil rights
Rights that promise equal opportunities and fair treatment for all people regardless of their race, sex, gender, religion, or nationality

Civil War
A war fought in America from 1861 to 1865, between Americans in northern states and Americans in southern states, primarily over the issue of slavery.

Colored
An outdated word for Black people, considered offensive today. It can be used when talking about history or referring to organizations like the National Association for the Advancement of Colored People.

Culture
The beliefs and ways of life of a group of people

Equality
Treatment that is the same for all people

Injustice
Unfair treatment

Jazz
A music form with roots in the American South

Landlord
A person who owns houses and rents them to others

Movement
People working together for a cause they believe in

Negro
An outdated word for Black people, which can be considered offensive today. It can be used when talking about history or referring to organizations like the Negro Leagues.

Protest
To express pain, unhappiness, or dissatisfaction about a situation

Racism
Unfair treatment because of one's skin color or race

Roots
The history or origin of a culture, a practice, or a person's family

Sculptor
An artist who makes three-dimensional art

Segregation
Separation of people by their race or skin color

Slavery
The practice of owning people and forcing them to work without pay

Unity
A state of togetherness, particularly in thoughts or ideas

Index

Abdul-Jabbar, Kareem   43
Armstrong, Louis   32
Bailey, Ruby   41
Baker, Josephine   34
baseball   36–37
basketball   38–39, 43
Bearden, Romare   29
Bechet, Sidney   32
"Black is beautiful" phrase   19
Black Lives Matter   43
blues music   22, 32
civil rights movement   33, 34, 35, 43
Cotton Club   31
dance and music   6, 22, 30–35, 43
Douglas, Aaron   28
Du Bois, W. E. B.   17, 23
Dutch settlers   10
East St. Louis, Illinois   16
Ellington, Duke   31
equal rights   33, 34, 35, 43
fashion   40–41
Garvey, Marcus   19, 27
Great Migration   12, 14
history of Harlem   10–12
Holiday, Billie   33
Hughes, Langston   6–7, 22–23

Hurston, Zora Neale   23, 43
Isaacs, John   38
jazz music   6, 30, 33
Johnson, James Weldon   35
Jones, Loïs Mailou   28
Kennedy, Jackie   41
King, Martin Luther, Jr.   34
Lawrence, Jacob   12, 25
Lenape people   10
Leonard, Buck   36
Lloyd, John Henry "Pop"   37
Locke, Alain   20
Lowe, Ann   41
Mills, Florence   6, 35
Moss, Thomas   18
Motley, Archibald   20
music and dance   6, 22, 30–35, 43
National Association for the Advancement of Colored People (NAACP)   17, 18, 31, 42
Negro League (baseball)   36, 37
Newsome, Effie Lee   24
Payton, Philip A., Jr.   14
Queen Latifah   43
racial tensions and violence   16, 18

racism   8–9, 14, 25, 34
   see also segregation
Renaissance (Europe)   8
Savage, Augusta   26
Schomburg, Arturo Alfonso   24
segregation   8–9, 15, 17, 31, 36, 41 see also racism
sharecropping   13
Smith, Bessie   32, 43
sports   36–39, 43
Stark, James   36
"Strange Fruit" (Holiday song)   33
subway trains   15
Trice, Edith   39
Universal Negro Improvement Association (UNIA)   19, 27
Van Der Zee, James   27, 39
visual art   25–29
voting rights   18
Walker, Alice   43
Walker, Madam C. J.   40
Wells-Barnett, Ida B.   18
Wilson, Woodrow   17
women's rights   18
women's sports   39
writers   6–7, 21–24, 43

Quiz

Answer the questions to see what you have learned. Check your answers in the key below.

1. What does Renaissance mean?
2. How did Philip Payton Jr. help Black people in Harlem?
3. Which Harlem Renaissance writer collected stories?
4. What sports were popular during the Harlem Renaissance?
5. During what two decades did the Harlem Renaissance mostly take place?

1. Rebirth 2. He rented houses to them 3. Zora Neale Hurston
4. Basketball and baseball 5. The 1920s and 1930s